THE FIRST LADY
OF THE
45TH & 47TH
PRESIDENCIES

THE FIRST LADY OF THE 45TH & 47TH PRESIDENCIES

A Heart of Love and Compassion in Public Life

By
Joe Hung Nguyen

Dedication

To the First Lady Melania Trump,
whose strength spoke without noise,
whose grace endured without retreat,
and whose love chose works over words.

> *You are an angel*
> *beauty in the soul, lovely in the heart.*
> *A gift from God, entrusted to children,*
> *and to all who learn from quiet goodness.*

And to the children—
not only of America, but of the world:
those seen and unseen, protected and endangered,
hopeful and hurting, known by name and known only to
God.

May they be sheltered in dignity,
formed in truth,
and raised in courage.

May their innocence be preserved,
their voices respected,
and their futures guarded by those entrusted with authority.

This book is dedicated to the belief that
the measure of a society is found
not in its power,
but in how faithfully it protects its children.

Amen.

Preface

A Testimony of Quiet Strength

Before history is written in headlines, it is lived in habits. Before legacy is debated, it is formed in choices made without witnesses. This book begins from that understanding—that some lives are not meant to be explained loudly, but received attentively. What follows is offered not as judgment, defense, or persuasion, but as a careful act of recognition: an attempt to notice strength where it is often overlooked, and to honor a form of leadership that speaks most clearly through restraint.

This book is not written in response to controversy, nor as an exercise in admiration. It is written as a **testimony**.

History often measures influence by volume—by how loudly one speaks, how frequently one appears, how insistently one asserts presence. Yet the most enduring forms of leadership have rarely followed that path. They are formed in discipline, sustained by restraint, and revealed through works rather than words. They belong to an older wisdom, one that understands that character is proven over time, and love is known by what it does.

Melania Trump stands within this tradition.

From her earliest years in Central Europe to her service as First Lady of the United States, her life reflects an uncommon consistency of mind and spirit. She did not reinvent herself to meet the demands of public fashion, nor did she allow circumstance to erode her sense of order and dignity. Her intelligence was shaped by preparation, her grace by self-command, and her strength by an inward clarity that did not require explanation.

This book does not ask the reader to suspend judgment, nor to overlook the complexities of the age in which she lived. It asks something both simpler and more demanding: to recognize **character when it appears quietly**, and to honor **service when it resists spectacle**.

As First Lady, Melania Trump approached her role not as a platform for self-expression, but as a responsibility entrusted to her—particularly toward children, families, and those who serve the nation.

Her *BE BEST* initiative was not conceived as a slogan, but as a moral posture: that children deserve protection, that virtue must be cultivated early, and that responsibility is learned through example rather than instruction alone.

In this, her work echoes the words of Christ:

> *"Whoever believes in Me will do the works that I do."* (John 14:12)

Love, in this light, is not measured by what one says,

nor by what one cites or recites.

*It is revealed in what one **does**—in actions*

that quietly declare, I truly love you, wholeheartedly and without condition.

True love moves mountains not by force, but by fidelity.

It brightens hope, gives birth to forgiveness,

softens hearts hardened by fear,

bridges differences, exalts peace,

and brings light where darkness has taken hold.

It is within this understanding of love as action that Melania Trump's mission as First Lady finds its clearest meaning.

Her work was neither performative nor reactive. It was preservative—seeking to guard innocence, affirm dignity, and sustain joy, especially among the young. As she herself expressed with clarity and resolve:

> *"I remain committed to helping children everywhere feel safe, seen, and supported. That is my mission."*

Such a mission does not require applause. It requires perseverance.

Throughout her public life, Melania Trump chose restraint over retaliation, composure over contention, and silence over display.

In an era that rewards immediacy and outrage, she practiced patience. In a culture that confuses exposure with authenticity, she preserved privacy—most notably in her devotion as a mother. Her love for her son was not curated for public approval; it was protected, formed, and lived daily.

This is not absence. It is presence of a deeper kind.

As wife, mother, immigrant, and First Lady, she bore responsibilities that demanded endurance rather than acclaim. She stood beside her husband through seasons of triumph and trial, not by competing for attention, but by remaining steady—faithful, disciplined, and resolute. Such strength rarely announces itself. It reveals itself over time.

The chapters that follow trace her journey from modest beginnings to global visibility, not to elevate her beyond measure, but to place her within a long moral lineage of women whose influence is known not by noise, but by steadfastness. Hers is a life that reminds us that elegance is a form of discipline, that intelligence does not require exhibition, and that love—especially love for children—is most powerful when it is practiced rather than proclaimed.

May this testimony invite the reader to reconsider how greatness often appears: quietly, faithfully, and through works that endure.

Amen.

Author's Note

This book was written with deliberate restraint.

It is not intended to persuade, defend, or respond to public debate. It does not attempt to interpret events exhaustively or to settle questions shaped by opinion and immediacy. Instead, it seeks to record a form of presence that is often overlooked: strength expressed through self-command, dignity sustained without display, and care shown through works rather than words.

As an immigrant who came to the United States seeking opportunity and belonging, I have long been attentive to the ways character is formed quietly—through discipline, faith, and responsibility accepted without demand for recognition. In Melania Trump's public life, I recognized a continuity of these virtues, particularly in her devotion to children, family, and moral order.

The reflections that follow were composed with care to avoid spectacle. Scriptural references and original poetry are included sparingly, not as commentary, but as moments of pause—offered in the spirit of contemplation rather than instruction. Wherever possible, the subject has been allowed to speak through example rather than interpretation.

This work is offered as a testimony, not a conclusion. It is written with respect for the reader's judgment and with the hope that what endures most clearly is not the author's voice, but the quiet strength of a life lived with intention.

— Joe Hung Nguyen
Deacon; refugee from Vietnam

Children,

Children,
Pure as moonlight upon the still lakake,
Innocent and radiant as blossoms newly born.
O fragrant buds of untainted beauty,
Scattering grace across a weary world,
Sowing joy amid hardship,
Soothing hearts worn by sorrow.
Children are the dawn of tomorrow,
Laughter ringing like hymns of hope,
Eyes bright enough to guide humanity
may yet know peace.

—Deacon Joé Hung Nguyen

Contents

Front Matter

Back Matter

"Our strength, as a nation, comes from our diversity and we should celebrate our differences to make us stronger and kinder."

– Melania Trump

Chapter One

Roots of Character

Before the world knew her name, there was a child shaped by order, silence, and work.

Melania Knauss was born in Novo Mesto, in what was then Yugoslavia, and raised in the small town of Sevnica—a place defined not by spectacle, but by rhythm. Life there moved according to seasons, routines, and responsibilities. In such places, character is not announced; it is formed. One learns early that beauty must be tended, that discipline is a companion to freedom, and that dignity begins at home.

Her family life reflected these values. There was an emphasis on craftsmanship, appearance without excess, and respect for effort. Clothing was not merely worn; it was cared for. Words were not scattered freely; they were chosen. Silence was not emptiness, but space—a place where thought and self-command could grow. These early habits would later become hallmarks of her public presence, though they were first learned in private.

From a young age, Melania exhibited a keen sense of observation. She noticed proportion, harmony, and detail

—qualities that would later draw her toward design and architecture. She learned languages with care, understanding that words are bridges between worlds. This intellectual discipline was not imposed for recognition, but cultivated as preparation.

In this, her education served not as display, but as foundation. The Europe of her youth valued form and restraint. Beauty was not meant to overwhelm, but to endure. Elegance was measured by balance, not excess. Such an environment quietly teaches that one need not dominate a room to belong within it. Presence, when rooted in self-respect, speaks without effort.

Faith, too, was present—not as performance, but as inheritance. It lived in gestures rather than declarations, in reverence rather than rhetoric. Like many formed within Catholic tradition, Melania learned that belief is not proven by volume, but by fidelity: showing up, enduring, keeping one's word. These lessons would later echo through her life as wife, mother, and First Lady.

There is a temptation in biography to rush toward the extraordinary—to seek early signs of destiny. Yet the truth is often simpler and more demanding. What prepared Melania Trump for public life was not ambition, but **formation**. She learned order before applause, responsibility before recognition, and discipline before opportunity.

Scripture reminds us that growth often happens unseen:

> *"Jesus went down with them and came to Nazareth, and was obedient to them."* (Luke 2:51)

Nazareth was not a place of renown. Neither was Sevnica. Yet it is in such places that the habits of the heart are shaped —habits that later withstand scrutiny, misunderstanding, and pressure.

When Melania would one day step onto global stages, she would bring with her these quiet foundations. She would not need to invent dignity; she had lived it. She would not need to learn restraint; it had been taught early. And she would not mistake attention for purpose, because purpose had already been formed long before attention arrived.

The roots of her character were deep, and therefore able to endure.

Chapter 2

Discipline of the Mind

Intelligence, when genuine, seeks order before expression. It prepares itself quietly, long before it is called upon to speak.

Melania Trump's intellectual formation followed this older understanding. Her education was not pursued as a means of exhibition, but as a discipline—one that trained the mind to observe, to measure, and to respect structure. From her early schooling through her university studies, she approached learning with seriousness, patience, and restraint. Knowledge, for her, was not an accessory; it was a responsibility.

Her academic interests led her toward architecture and design, fields that demand both imagination and precision. Architecture, in particular, teaches a reverence for proportion. Every line must serve a purpose. Every structure must bear weight. Beauty is not imposed upon a space; it arises from harmony, balance, and respect for limits. These principles, learned early, would later echo in her personal style and public demeanor.

Language became another instrument of discipline. Melania learned to move between cultures through words, mastering multiple languages with care and humility. Multilingualism shaped not only her communication, but her understanding of people. To speak another language is to step outside oneself, to listen before responding, and to acknowledge that meaning is never owned by one voice alone.

Such habits cultivate interior order. They teach patience, attentiveness, and self-command—qualities increasingly rare in public life. In a world that rewards immediacy, she learned to wait. In a culture that equates confidence with volume, she practiced clarity through restraint.

This intellectual formation also shaped her independence. Education gave her the confidence to navigate unfamiliar environments without surrendering identity. She did not rely on imitation, nor did she seek validation through conformity. Her sense of self was anchored in preparation rather than approval.

There is a moral dimension to disciplined thought. Scripture reminds us:

> *"For God is not a God of disorder but of peace."*
> (1 Corinthians 14:33)

Order of mind fosters peace of spirit. It allows one to stand firm amid confusion and to respond thoughtfully rather than reactively. This interior steadiness would later become visible in moments of public scrutiny, when silence proved more eloquent than argument.

Education, in this sense, was not a ladder to prominence, but a safeguard of integrity. It protected her from the temptation to perform intellect rather than live it. It taught her that wisdom often appears understated, and that true understanding is proven by consistency over time.

By the time Melania entered professional life, her mind had already been trained to value structure, discernment, and purpose. These were not skills acquired for attention; they were disciplines embraced for life.

Chapter 3

Beauty with Boundaries

Beauty, when disciplined, becomes a form of testimony.

Melania Trump's entry into the world of modeling did not arise from indulgence, nor from a desire for spectacle. It emerged naturally from her physical grace, composure, and sense of proportion—qualities already formed through upbringing and education. Yet what distinguished her path was not appearance alone, but the manner in which she carried herself within an industry often marked by excess and exploitation.

From the outset, she approached modeling as a profession. Work required preparation, punctuality, and restraint. She understood that success demanded seriousness rather than self-display, and that boundaries were not obstacles to opportunity, but safeguards of integrity. In an environment where attention is often mistaken for worth, she maintained a clear separation between vocation and identity.

Her professionalism earned respect. Designers and photographers recognized her reliability, her discipline, and her refusal to compromise dignity for notoriety. She did not cultivate scandal, nor did she seek controversy as currency. Instead, she allowed her work to speak through consistency and presence. This approach, though quieter, proved enduring.

There is a misconception that modesty diminishes strength. In truth, it refines it. By choosing restraint, Melania preserved autonomy in an industry that frequently seeks to define women by surface alone. She did not permit herself to be reduced to an image, nor did she allow her work to eclipse her interior life.

Scripture offers a timeless reminder:

> *"Charm is deceptive, and beauty is fleeting; but a woman who fears the Lord is to be praised."*
> (Proverbs 31:30)

This is not a dismissal of beauty, but a reordering of it. Beauty finds its proper place when it serves truth rather than vanity, purpose rather than provocation. In Melania's case, it became an expression of discipline—measured, intentional, and dignified.

Her years in modeling also strengthened her independence. She traveled, negotiated contracts, and sustained herself through effort rather than reliance. These experiences sharpened discernment and resilience. They taught her how to navigate public spaces without surrendering private principles.

It is worth noting that she did not use her profession as a platform for commentary or self-definition. She allowed silence to protect substance. This choice, though often misunderstood, revealed a confidence rooted not in approval, but in self-respect.

In later years, critics would attempt to rewrite this chapter of her life according to fashionable narratives. Yet the truth remains plain: she conducted herself with boundaries intact, dignity preserved, and purpose uncorrupted.

Beauty, when governed by discipline, does not distract from character—it reveals it.

Chapter 4

New York

Immigrant Courage and Independence

New York has long been the first chapter in America's unfolding promise—a city where lawful arrival, honest work, and quiet perseverance form the foundation of lasting success. For **Melania Trump**, her journey to New York was marked not by spectacle, but by courage grounded in discipline and respect for the law. She came not to demand opportunity, but to earn it.

Her arrival in America followed the proper path. She respected the nation she sought to join, honoring its laws and customs while bringing with her the values shaped by her European upbringing: order, restraint, and personal responsibility. This lawful beginning mattered. It reflected a deeper truth—that genuine freedom is sustained by structure, and that opportunity flourishes where rules are honored, not bypassed.

"I came to America for my dreams."
—Melania Trump

Those dreams were neither abstract nor entitled. They were shaped by patience, self-command, and the willingness to stand on one's own. Independence was not a slogan, but a daily discipline.

The Immigrant's Test

New York does not soften its edges for newcomers. It tests resolve daily. In this city of unrelenting pace and expectation, Melania embraced independence. She worked, supported herself, and learned to navigate a demanding environment without complaint. There was no presumption of favor in her approach—only effort. Each step forward was earned through professionalism, consistency, and quiet determination.

Her perseverance echoed the experience of generations before her—immigrants who arrived with skill, humility, and resolve, trusting that America rewards those willing to contribute rather than consume. She did not seek shortcuts. She accepted uncertainty, understanding that dignity is forged through patience and endurance.

The American Promise, Quietly Fulfilled

The American promise is often misunderstood as loud success or sudden recognition. In truth, it is fulfilled quietly: through lawful work, personal growth, and the freedom to build a life with one's own hands. Melania's New York years embodied this deeper promise. She advanced step by step, not abandoning her identity, but refining it within the framework of American opportunity.

Her independence was not a rejection of community, but a prerequisite for it. By standing on her own, she earned her place. In a city that rewards resilience more than rhetoric, she demonstrated that true assimilation does not erase one's roots—it strengthens them through responsibility and respect.

A Journey of Faith and Resolve

Her journey bears a timeless parallel to the biblical account of Abraham, who was called to leave what was familiar and step forward in faith, trusting a path not yet fully revealed. Such journeys are not marked by certainty, but by obedience, endurance, and courage shaped by purpose rather than fear.

Like Abraham's, Melania's path required leaving comfort behind, embracing uncertainty, and moving forward with resolve grounded not in entitlement, but in trust—trust in effort, in order, and in the promise that faithfulness yields fruit in its proper time.

Strength Without Noise

In an era that often celebrates provocation, Melania chose composure. She understood that independence is not announced; it is lived. New York taught her how to remain steady amid scrutiny, how to preserve inner order while surrounded by chaos. These lessons, formed in anonymity, would later sustain her under global attention.

Her immigrant story stands as a reminder of what America has always represented at its best: a nation where lawful entry, hard work, and moral discipline open doors not through favor, but through merit. This is the enduring promise that built New York—and the country itself.

A Foundation for the Future

New York was more than a city of arrival; it was a proving ground. It affirmed that courage does not always raise its voice, and independence does not require rebellion. For Melania, the city refined her belief that success rooted in legality, effort, and character endures long after applause fades.

Her journey through New York reflects a timeless American truth: when one comes with respect for the law, willingness to work, and confidence tempered by humility, the promise of America is not merely imagined—it is fulfilled.

Chapter 5

Meeting Donald Trump
Partnership, Not Ornament

History often misreads strength. It assumes that presence must be loud and influence must be visible. The meeting of Melania and Donald J. Trump challenges that modern error. Their union was not one of ornament and display, but of partnership—distinct roles joined by mutual respect, balance, and shared resolve.

Courtship Rooted in Respect

Their courtship unfolded deliberately, not hastily. Donald Trump, already a figure of commanding public presence, encountered in Melania something uncommon in his world: composure without calculation, confidence without rivalry. She did not seek to impress by imitation, nor did she diminish herself to please. She stood firmly as herself.

Melania, in turn, recognized in Donald a man of decisive

action and unrelenting vision. She understood that leadaership carries weight, scrutiny, and sacrifice. Rather than compete with his public role, she respected it. Their relationship matured through honest exchange, clear boundaries, and mutual admiration—qualities too often absent in modern portrayals of power.

Marriage, when it came, was not a transformation of identity but a confirmation of it. Melania did not disappear into her husband's shadow, nor did she demand the spotlight. She entered the marriage as an equal in dignity, bringing steadiness where there was momentum, and discernment where there was drive.

Strength, Balance, and Complementarity

The strength of their partnership lay in contrast properly ordered. Donald Trump's boldness required balance; Melania's restraint provided it. His public force needed an inner anchor; her presence supplied calm and perspective. This was not competition, but completion.

Modern culture often mistakes equality for sameness. Their marriage illustrates a more enduring truth: harmony arises when strengths are complementary rather than duplicated. Melania did not measure her worth by volume or visibility. She understood that influence often operates quietly, shaping decisions through counsel, steadiness, and moral clarity.

Refusal to Be Merely Symbolic

From the beginning, Melania resisted being reduced to symbolism. She refused to be a decorative figure or a borrowed voice. Her independence, formed long before marriage, remained intact. She spoke when purpose required it and remained silent when silence carried greater dignity.

This refusal was not defiance; it was wisdom. She understood that lasting authority comes from authenticity, not performance. In a public world eager to assign roles, she defined her own—supportive without submission, loyal without erasure.

Key Insight

A strong man needs a woman who does not compete—but completes.

This principle, timeless and often forgotten, defined their union. Melania's strength did not challenge Donald Trump's leadership; it steadied it. Her presence was not ornamental but essential, not performative but formative.

Their partnership stands as a reminder that the most enduring alliances are not built on rivalry or display, but on respect, trust, and complementary strength. In choosing partnership over ornament, Melania affirmed a traditional truth with modern relevance: greatness is sustained not by echoing power, but by balancing it with wisdom.

"Comforting
children was
one of the most
rewarding aspects
of my role as
First Lady."

—*Melania Trump*

Chapter 6

Motherhood:
Raising Barron with Intention

In a world that rewards exposure, Melania Trump chose devotion. Motherhood, for her, was never a public performance but a sacred responsibility—one requiring presence, protection, and intentional moral formation. From the moment Barron was born, she understood that the most important work of her life would be carried out quietly, beyond the reach of applause.

> *"My first priority is being a mother."*
> —Melania Trump

These words were not a slogan; they were a rule of life.

Private Devotion, Public Restraint

Melania's devotion to Barron was marked by attentiveness rather than display. She guarded his routines, his education, and his inner life with deliberate care. In an age that often confuses visibility with love, she embraced restraint. She knew that a child does not need an audience—he needs stability, affection, and moral clarity.

Her commitment to privacy was not avoidance but protection. She recognized that childhood, once surrendered to public consumption, cannot be reclaimed. By shielding Barron from unnecessary exposure, she preserved for him the freedom to grow without the distortions of constant scrutiny.

Protection from the Noise of the World

The modern media environment is relentless, especially for children born into prominence. Melania understood this danger early and acted decisively. She drew firm boundaries between public life and private motherhood, ensuring that Barron's development was guided by family values rather than external pressure.

This protection required strength. It meant resisting demands for access, refusing to exploit her child for image or narrative, and enduring criticism in silence. Such restraint is rarely celebrated, yet it reflects a deeper courage —the courage to place a child's well-being above one's own public standing.

Moral Formation Over Applause

For Melania, success in motherhood was not measured by headlines but by character. She emphasized discipline, respect, and personal responsibility. She understood that moral formation precedes achievement, and that a child shaped by values will stand firm long after attention fades.

By choosing intention over indulgence, she reaffirmed a

traditional truth: children are not extensions of their parents' ambition, but souls entrusted to their care. Her role was not to showcase Barron, but to prepare him.

Gospel Reflection: Mary's Silent Guardianship

Melania's approach to motherhood finds a quiet parallel in the Gospel image of Mary, who guarded her Son not through spectacle, but through faithful presence:

> *"But Mary treasured up all these things and pondered them in her heart."*
> —Luke 2:19

Mary did not seek recognition for her role. She watched, protected, and remained steadfast. Her strength lay in silence, her influence in constancy. In a similar way, Melania's motherhood was defined by presence without display—by the wisdom to know when love is best expressed through quiet guardianship.

A Legacy Formed in Silence

History often overlooks the unseen labor of mothers, yet it is there that futures are formed. By raising Barron with intention, Melania affirmed that the most enduring legacies are built not in public arenas, but in the patient, faithful work of home.

Her motherhood stands as a reminder—especially in unsettled times—that protection, discipline, and moral clarity are acts of love. In choosing devotion over display, she honored an ancient truth: the strongest foundations are laid in silence.

◆

Chapter 7

Becoming First Lady: Grace Under Fire

The transition into the White House has always been a passage marked by scrutiny. For Melania Trump, it became something more severe: a trial by fire. Entering one of the most visible roles in the world, she did so not as a seeker of applause, but as a woman resolved to remain anchored in her values amid unrelenting pressure.

The title of First Lady carries expectations shaped by fashion, performance, and public approval. Melania accepted the responsibility, but not the distortion. She understood that the role was honorary, not theatrical— meant to serve, not to entertain. From the beginning, she chose order over chaos and substance over spectacle.

A Difficult Passage into Public Life

The move into the White House was neither simple nor ceremonial. It demanded adjustment, sacrifice, and careful protection of family life. Melania approached this transition with deliberation, prioritizing stability for her son while adapting to the demands of national attention. Her decisions reflected prudence rather than impulse—an approach consistent with her lifelong discipline.

Rather than rushing to satisfy external expectations, she moved at a pace guided by responsibility. In doing so, she affirmed a traditional principle often forgotten in public life: leadership begins with stewardship, especially within one's own household.

Media Hostility and Misrepresentation

From the outset, Melania faced persistent hostility and frequent misrepresentation. Her words were scrutinized, her silence distorted, and her intentions questioned. In an era that rewards provocation, her restraint was treated as weakness. Yet restraint, rightly understood, is a form of strength.

She was judged not by her actions alone, but by narratives imposed upon her. Instead of responding in kind, she endured. She understood that public vindication is fleeting, but personal integrity endures. By refusing to mirror hostility, she denied it power.

> *"I stay true to myself and my values."*
> —Melania Trump

These words reveal the inner discipline that guided her conduct. She chose to govern herself before attempting to answer others.

Dignity Over Retaliation

In the face of repeated provocation, Melania declined retaliation. She did not weaponize her platform, nor did she indulge in public grievance. Her silence was not surrender; it was discernment. She recognized that dignity, once lost, cannot be reclaimed through argument.

This choice reflected an older moral wisdom—that character is revealed not in triumph, but under pressure. By maintaining composure, she modeled a rare form of leadership: self-command in the midst of attack.

Scriptural Anchor

The endurance she displayed finds resonance in Scripture:

> *"When He was reviled, He did not revile in return; when He suffered, He did not threaten, but entrusted Himself to Him who judges justly."*
> —1 Peter 2:23

This passage captures the heart of Melania's response. Rather than seeking immediate vindication, she entrusted her reputation to time, truth, and conscience. Such restraint does not invite attention—but it commands respect.

Grace Forged in Trial

Grace is not softness; it is strength refined by trial. Melania's tenure as First Lady demonstrated that dignity can withstand hostility, and that silence, when chosen wisely, can speak louder than outrage.

In choosing grace under fire, she offered a counterexample to a culture addicted to reaction. Her conduct affirmed a lasting truth: when values are secure, retaliation is unnecessary. True grace endures—not because it escapes criticism, but because it rises above it.

"The well-being of children is the most important responsibility."

–Melania Trump

Chapter 8

BE BEST

Children as Trust, the Heart of a Legacy

If public life tests endurance, legacy is revealed in what one chooses to protect.

Throughout her time as First Lady, Melania Trump returned again and again to one unwavering priority: children. In an era dominated by outrage and performance, she chose stewardship. BE BEST was not a response to criticism, nor a gesture for approval. It was the natural extension of her character—formed through motherhood, strengthened through trial, and expressed through quiet service.

Melania understood a truth as old as civilization itself: **the future is entrusted, not inherited**. Children are not political symbols, nor instruments of ambition. They are

"No child should ever feel hungry, stalked, frightened, terrorized, bullied, isolated or afraid, with nowhere to turn."

– First Lady Melania Trump, September 2017

lives in formation—fragile, impressionable, and deserving of protection long before they are asked to perform, conform, or compete.

Children as Moral Trust

BE BEST addressed what most directly shapes a child's inner world: dignity, responsibility, and safety. Its focus was deliberate and restrained—anti-bullying, online protection, emotional well-being, and care for the most vulnerable. These were not fashionable causes. They were necessary ones.

Rather than moralizing from a distance, Melania listened. Rather than demanding attention, she showed presence. She worked within schools, hospitals, and communities where the stakes were real and the rewards invisible. Her concern was not how initiatives appeared, but whether they endured.

In this, she affirmed a traditional understanding of leadership: **to protect what cannot protect itself is the highest form of authority**.

A Quiet Mirror of Her Vision

"Be Best."
Simple in language, demanding in practice.

This phrase was never intended as branding, nor as a slogan for applause. It was guidance—calling children, families, and society toward responsibility, dignity, and moral formation. Its strength lies in its clarity; its endurance lies in its intention.

In choosing these words, Melania Trump affirmed an enduring truth: that character is formed through discipline, kindness, and effort, not entitlement. BE BEST did not promise ease. It called for aspiration shaped by responsibility and compassion anchored in action.

What made the phrase powerful was not repetition, but consistency. It reflected how she lived, how she served, and how she understood the future entrusted to the young.

The moral vision behind BE BEST can be understood not through slogans, but through reflection.

Children

Children,
Pure as moonlight upon the still lake,
Innocent and radiant as blossoms newly born.
O fragrant buds of untainted beauty,
Scattering grace across a weary world,
Sowing joy amid hardship,
Soothing hearts worn by sorrow.

Children are the dawn of tomorrow,
Laughter ringing like hymns of hope,
Eyes bright enough to guide humanity,
Guarding innocence so the world may yet know peace.

—*Deacon Joe Hung Nguyen*

This poem does not speak *for* Melania Trump; it reflects

what she quietly lived. Her work for children was rooted in the conviction that innocence must be guarded before it is lost, and character formed before power is granted.

Service Without Spectacle

BE BEST was often misunderstood precisely because it refused theatrics. It did not trade in outrage or accusation. It sought formation, not confrontation. In a culture accustomed to noise, its restraint was mistaken for absence.

Yet Melania's service followed an older ethic: **What matters most is rarely done before an audience.**

She visited without cameras, supported without self-promotion, and persisted without complaint. She did not answer dismissal with anger, nor criticism with performance. She allowed the work to stand on its own, trusting that what is done for children bears fruit beyond the news cycle.

Scriptural Anchor

The spirit of BE BEST finds resonance in Scripture:

> *"But when you give to the needy, do not let your left hand know what your right hand is doing... and your Father who sees in secret will reward you."*
> —Matthew 6:3–4

This passage does not glorify obscurity for its own sake; it sanctifies intention. It reminds us that the worth of an act is not measured by attention received, but by good accomplished.

The Enduring Measure of a First Lady

Titles fade. Controversies pass. Applause dissolves.
But children grow.

In choosing to center her public service on their well-being, Melania Trump chose the longest view of history. She invested not in headlines, but in human formation. She understood that a nation's strength is not revealed in how it treats the powerful, but in how it guards the young.

BE BEST was not her loudest work.
It was her truest.

And because children endure, **so does her legacy**.

Chapter 9

Works, Not Noise: A First Lady of Action

Public life often confuses visibility with virtue. In recent years, activism has increasingly been measured by volume—by statements issued, slogans repeated, and attention commanded. Melania Trump chose a different path. She believed that values are best revealed not through declaration, but through action.

"I prefer to show my values through my work."
—Melania Trump

This conviction shaped her conduct as First Lady and defined her service beyond the spotlight. While others sought to dominate the conversation, she chose to meet real needs quietly and consistently.

Service to Those Who Serve

Among Melania Trump's most steadfast commitments was her support for military families. She recognized that service to the nation does not end on the battlefield; it extends into homes shaped by sacrifice, uncertainty, and resilience.

Her visits with military families were marked by attentiveness rather than ceremony. She listened more than she spoke. She honored their sacrifices without politicizing them. In doing so, she affirmed a traditional understanding of patriotism—one rooted not in rhetoric, but in respect for duty faithfully carried.

Her receipt of the **Patriot Award** reflected this same ethic. It was not sought, nor was it exploited for attention. It stood as recognition of a First Lady who understood that national strength depends on those willing to serve quietly, often without public acknowledgment.

Presence Without Performance

Melania's hospital visits revealed another dimension of her approach to service. She met with children, families, and patients not as a public figure performing compassion, but as a human being offering presence. These visits were often conducted away from cameras, without press statements or curated images.

Such restraint ran counter to modern expectations. Yet it reflected moral clarity. Compassion, she understood, does not require witnesses to be sincere. The dignity of those suffering must not be subordinated to the visibility of those helping.

In these moments, her service was personal, not performative. It was shaped by empathy rather than narrative, and by respect rather than display.

Unseen Charity, Enduring Effect

Much of Melania Trump's work will never appear in headlines. It was carried out in private conversations, handwritten notes, quiet encouragement, and sustained attention to those overlooked by public discourse. This unseen charity was not incidental—it was intentional.

She resisted the impulse to turn generosity into content. Instead, she honored an older moral standard: that good done for its own sake carries greater weight than good done for recognition.

In an age where visibility is often mistaken for virtue, her restraint served as a corrective. She demonstrated that service need not announce itself to be real, and that dignity flourishes where humility governs action.

Contrast: Action Versus Activism

The contrast between modern activism and Melania Trump's approach could not be clearer. Activism often seeks to persuade through volume; her service sought to help through presence. Activism frequently measures success by reaction; she measured it by effect.

She did not frame her work as resistance or performance. She framed it as responsibility. Her conduct reflected a belief that moral authority is earned through consistency, not asserted through outrage.

This difference is not stylistic—it is philosophical. It reflects a conviction that the most meaningful work is often done without applause, and that service loses its integrity when it becomes spectacle.

A Consistent Character

What unites Melania Trump's work for children, military families, and the vulnerable is not theme but character. In each case, she chose restraint over reaction, action over argument, and duty over display.

Her legacy is therefore not confined to a single initiative or moment. It is revealed in the pattern of her conduct—a pattern marked by discipline, compassion, and moral seriousness.

She did not seek to redefine the role of First Lady by expanding its visibility. She refined it by restoring its purpose.

Enduring Measure

When public noise fades, what remains is what was done.

Melania Trump's service stands as a reminder that action grounded in values endures longer than rhetoric shaped by fashion. By choosing work over noise, she affirmed a truth that transcends politics: **character expressed through service leaves a deeper mark than words ever can**.

In a time eager for performance, she chose purpose. And in doing so, she offered a model of leadership that speaks most clearly—by acting quietly and faithfully where it matters most.

Chapter 10

Faith, Silence, and Strength

Faith, when it is authentic, does not seek to be displayed. It forms the interior life quietly, disciplines the will, and reveals its power not through argument but through endurance. In the life of Melania Trump, faith was neither a public instrument nor a political signal. It was a private anchor—respected, protected, and lived without spectacle.

A Catholic Faith Treated with Reverence

Melania Trump's Catholic faith was approached with seriousness and restraint. She neither denied it nor exploited it. There were no grand declarations, no attempts to use belief as a shield or a weapon. Instead, her faith remained personal—expressed through conduct, modesty, and a sense of moral order.

Such reserve reflects an older understanding of belief: that what is sacred is not performed. Faith that seeks applause risks becoming hollow. By refusing to place her spiritual life on display, she preserved its dignity and avoided the distortions that arise when belief is subjected to public consumption or speculation.

Her faith informed her conscience, not her image.

The Discipline of Silence

In a culture that rewards immediate reaction, silence is often misunderstood. It is mistaken for passivity or fear. Yet silence can be one of the most disciplined responses available to a person under scrutiny. Melania Trump practiced silence deliberately—not as avoidance, but as control.

She did not answer every provocation. She did not feel compelled to correct every mischaracterization. She understood that constant response places one's inner life at the mercy of external noise. Silence, by contrast, preserves sovereignty of the self.

This discipline required strength. To remain quiet while being spoken about, judged, or misread demands self-command. It reflects confidence rooted not in approval, but in conviction.

The Power of Restraint

Restraint is strength ordered by wisdom. It is not the absence of feeling, but the mastery of it. Throughout her public life, Melania Trump demonstrated restraint in speech, appearance, and demeanor. Each choice reflected intention rather than impulse.

By limiting her words, she increased their weight. By refusing to engage in constant defense, she denied her critics control over her posture. Her restraint was not coldness; it was clarity. She understood that dignity, once surrendered, cannot be recovered through louder speech.

In an era drawn to excess, her measured presence stood apart.

Theological Reflection: Silence and Humility

Within Christian tradition, silence has long been understood as a source of authority rather than its absence. Scripture and spiritual teaching consistently affirm that humility precedes strength, and that self-mastery is the foundation of moral authority.

Christ Himself often responded to accusation with silence, entrusting judgment to truth rather than self-defense. The saints learned that humility does not weaken authority; it purifies it. To restrain one's response is not to yield ground, but to choose a higher ground.

Melania Trump's posture reflects this theological wisdom. By refusing to compete in noise, she retained clarity. By practicing humility, she exercised authority over herself—and that authority endured.

At the heart of such faith is not ambition, but a quiet hope for peace that reaches beyond the self.

A Wish

If God granted me one wish
neither I wish to be rich
nor famous
nor power
nor wise
I just wish peace to the world
and the unity to all His dispersed
children so they all may live
in harmony
happy, safety and joyfully
in God's love

A Wish

If God granted me one wish
neither I wish to be rich
nor famous
nor power
nor wise
I just wish peace to the world
and the unity to all His dispersed children
so they all may live in harmony
happy, safety and joyfully in God's love

(Deacon Joe Hung Nguyen)

Strength That Endures

Faith, silence, and strength are not separate virtues. They are integrated disciplines. Faith orders the soul. Silence protects it. Strength emerges from both.

Melania Trump's example offers a corrective to an age restless for attention. It reminds us that the most enduring strength is not loud, not reactive, and not theatrical. It is disciplined, grounded, and quietly resolute.

In choosing faith without display, silence without surrender, and restraint without weakness, she demonstrated a form of strength that does not fade—because it does not depend on the world's approval to stand.

We must find better
ways to honor and support
the basic goodness
of our children.

–First Lady Melania Trump

Chapter 11

Standing Beside the President

Public leadership is often judged by speeches and decisions. Far less visible is the weight borne by those who stand beside the leader—the steady presence required when scrutiny intensifies and trials multiply. For Melania Trump, loyalty was not performative. It was disciplined, deliberate, and carried with quiet resolve through seasons of sustained pressure.

Loyalty Under Trial

The presidency subjected the Trump family to relentless% challenge: political opposition, legal battles, and continuous public attack. In these trials, Melania Trump did not seek the spotlight, nor did she attempt to counter every accusation. Her loyalty was expressed through steadiness rather than display.

She understood that leadership under siege requires

stability at its core. To stand beside the President in such moments is not passive; it is costly. It demands composure when provocation is constant and endurance when outcomes are uncertain. Her support did not add noise to the storm. It provided ballast against it.

Support Without Theatrics

Modern expectations often confuse loyalty with spectacle. Melania rejected that distortion. She did not narrate her support or dramatize her role. Instead, she maintained a posture of calm presence—attentive, measured, and firm.

This restraint was purposeful. She recognized that theatrics can weaken rather than strengthen leadership by shifting focus from duty to drama. By remaining composed, she preserved the dignity of the office and the integrity of her own role. Her presence communicated resolve without a single raised voice.

The Unseen Burden of Leadership Families

Families of leaders carry burdens the public rarely sees: constant security concerns, invasive scrutiny, and the pressure of representing stability while absorbing uncertainty. These demands do not pause with the day's headlines; they persist quietly, shaping daily life.

Melania Trump bore these responsibilities with discretion. She protected family boundaries where possible and absorbed pressures without public complaint. Such endurance is seldom acknowledged, yet it is essential. Leadership is sustained not only by decision-makers, but by those who make endurance possible behind the scenes.

Her role exemplified a traditional truth: support offered in private often sustains outcomes achieved in public.

Biblical Parallel: Esther's Calling

Melania's posture during these trials finds a fitting parallel in the story of Esther—a woman positioned not for acclaim, but for purpose.

> *"And who knows whether you have not come to the kingdom for such a time as this?"*
> —Esther 4:14

Esther's strength was not expressed through constant speech, but through courage exercised at the right moment.

She carried risk silently, prepared carefully, and acted with restraint shaped by responsibility. Her position was not sought for vanity, but accepted for service.

In a similar way, Melania Trump occupied her place with awareness rather than ambition. She understood that presence itself can be decisive—that steadiness, when trials converge, is a form of action.

A Quiet Pillar

Standing beside the President required fortitude without recognition. It demanded loyalty without self-assertion and strength without spectacle. Melania Trump fulfilled this role not by competing for attention, but by providing continuity amid conflict.

Such loyalty does not announce itself, yet it endures. It is revealed not in moments of ease, but when pressure is sustained and criticism unrelenting. In those moments, her presence served as a quiet pillar—unseen by many, essential to the whole.

History often records the visible acts of leadership. It rarely notes the steadfast figures who make perseverance possible.

Yet without such figures, leadership falters. In standing beside the President through trial, Melania Trump demonstrated a loyalty defined not by words, but by unwavering resolve—exercised, like Esther's, **"for such a time as this."**

◆

CEREMORIAL PRESENCE

In her ceremonial presence. Melania Trump spoke without words, using elegance as her language. Her sartorial choices - were not just garments but symbols - each fabric, each color chosen with deliberation to speak of dignity and unity.

Chapter 12

Legacy of a First Lady

Legacies are not fashioned by momentary approval, but by enduring example. In an age marked by excess, reaction, and performance, Melania Trump offered something rarer and more lasting: restraint guided by principle. Her legacy as First Lady is not defined by novelty, but by restoration—of elegance, dignity, and purpose to a role often misunderstood.

Redefining Elegance

Elegance, rightly understood, is not ornament. It is order made visible. Melania Trump redefined elegance by refusing excess—of speech, of gesture, and of self-promotion. Her bearing communicated respect for the office she occupied and for the nation it represents.

She demonstrated that elegance is not about fashion alone, but about proportion and discipline. Each public appearance reflected deliberation rather than impulse.

In doing so, she reminded a restless culture that refinement is not weakness, but strength under control.

Restoring Dignity to the Role

The role of First Lady has, at times, been pulled toward performance or activism shaped by noise. Melania Trump resisted this drift. She restored dignity by treating the position as one of stewardship rather than spectacle.

Her initiatives were focused, her presence measured, and her voice used sparingly. She understood that the authority of the role is preserved not by constant assertion, but by consistency and restraint. By honoring the boundaries of the office, she strengthened it.

In choosing service over display, she reaffirmed the First Lady's role as a stabilizing force—one that supports, uplifts, and protects without overshadowing.

A Model for Future First Ladies

Melania Trump's example offers a model rooted in timeless principles rather than fleeting trends. She demonstrated that a First Lady need not mirror the political climate to remain relevant. Instead, relevance is achieved through integrity, composure, and devotion to what endures.

Future First Ladies may draw from her example the freedom to serve without imitation—to act without theatrics and to lead without noise. Her legacy affirms that influence can be exercised quietly and that dignity, once established, commands respect across generations.

Final Thought

Melania Trump reminds us that **virtue does not need permission to exist**.

It stands on its own, requiring neither applause nor approval. In a world eager for affirmation, her legacy offers a different lesson: that character shaped by restraint, faith, and service endures beyond the moment.

...Her legacy affirms that influence can be exercised quietly and that dignity, once established, commands respect across generations.

In placing children, dignity, and restraint at the center, she offered not a moment, but a model.

Such a legacy does not fade with time. It strengthens it.

Poetic Benediction

She walked with grace through halls of power,

Her silence spoke, her presence flowered.

A mother's love, a nation's guest,

Her legacy whispers: Be Best.

Whoever receives
one such child in
My name receives Me.

–Matthew 18:5

Epilogue

What Endures

History is often impatient. It seeks immediate judgment, clear verdicts, and simple narratives. Yet what endures is rarely revealed in the moment. It emerges slowly, after noise has faded and attention has moved on. The life and legacy of Melania Trump invite such patience.

She entered public life without seeking it, remained within it without being consumed by it, and departed it without clinging to applause. Through years of scrutiny, misunderstanding, and sustained pressure, she held a steady course shaped by restraint, faith, and duty. These qualities are not dramatic. They are durable.

Melania Trump's legacy is not found in the volume of her words, but in their measure. It is not defined by reaction, but by intention. In her devotion to family, her work for children, her quiet service to those who suffer, and her steadfast loyalty in times of trial, she demonstrated that dignity can be preserved even in the most demanding arenas.

She reminded the nation that elegance is not excess, that strength need not be loud, and that virtue does not require permission to exist. At a time when public life often rewards performance over principle, her example offered a different path—one rooted in self-command, humility, and moral clarity.

The initiatives she advanced, the lives she touched, and the standards she upheld will not always be catalogued in headlines. Yet their influence remains, carried forward in children protected, families supported, and a role restored to seriousness and grace.

Epilogues are not endings; they are moments of stillness. They ask not what was proclaimed, but what was shown. In Melania Trump's case, what was shown was a form of leadership shaped by restraint, sustained by faith, and exercised through service.

When history looks back with greater calm, it may find that her quiet consistency accomplished what louder gestures could not. For in the end, it is not noise that endures, but character—and character, once formed, leaves a mark that time itself cannot erase.

Cadence of Compassion

Compassion is not noise; it is rhythm.

In Melania Trump's life of public service, the nation encountered a cadence of mercy—gentle, steady, and unwavering. Her tone did not seek applause, but healing. She spoke softly, yet her presence carried weight, reminding a restless culture that love is action and compassion is strength.

This cadence aligns with the Lord's command:

> *"Whoever believes in me will do the works that I do."*
> —John 14:12

She did not merely advocate for kindness; she practiced it. Her presence in places of sorrow, her quiet comfort to grieving families, her steady encouragement to children— each became part of a rhythm of restoration. It was not hurried. It was faithful.

Her Healing Rhythm

- **Emotional clarity** — sincerity without spectacle
- **Gentle presence** — comfort offered without fanfare
- **Consistent mercy** — steadiness even in storms
- **Enduring legacy** — compassion as balm for the nation's wounds

Poetic Benediction

A cadence soft, yet strong and true,
Compassion's rhythm in all she'd do.
No boast, no wrath, no worldly claim,
Just mercy's pulse in love's pure name.

"We must teach each child
the value of empathy
and communication that are
at the core of kindness,
mindfulness, integrity, and
leadership."

—First Lady Melania Trump, *September 2017*

Acknowledgements

This book exists because of my beloved wife, Maria

For more than fifty-three years, she has lived a life defined not by words, but by action. Through discipline, focus, and perseverance, she built her own business, provided education for our children, secured stability for our family, and worked steadily toward the future with determination and care. She spoke little of her efforts, preferring instead to complete the work set before her.

Her devotion to family, her quiet strength, and her lifelong commitment to responsibility made this book possible. In her way of living—measured, faithful, and resolute—I recognized the same virtues this book seeks to honor.

For a life shared, a family sustained, and a partnership grounded in action, I give my sincere thanks.

Back Matter

Selected Quotes of Melania Trump

Words spoken sparingly often carry greater weight. Melania Trump never sought to define herself through constant commentary; instead, she allowed carefully chosen words to reflect deeply held convictions.

Melania Trump spoke rarely and deliberately. Her words were not issued to dominate conversation, but to clarify values. The following selections are arranged thematically, allowing her voice to reveal the moral consistency that shaped her work as First Lady.

◆ On Children and Compassion

"The well-being of children is the most important responsibility."

This conviction formed the foundation of BE BEST. It reflects a belief that public life ultimately answers to the needs of the young, and that no political aim outweighs the duty to protect innocence and foster growth.

> *"We must find better ways to honor and support the basic goodness of our children, especially in social media."*

Here, she identified a modern challenge without moral panic. Rather than condemning technology, she emphasized responsibility—calling adults to guide, protect, and form rather than exploit or abandon.

> *"Children and teenagers can be fragile. They are hurt when they are made fun of or made to feel less in looks or intelligence."*

This statement reveals her attentiveness to unseen wounds. It underscores her insistence that dignity must be safeguarded early, before cruelty hardens and confidence is lost.

> *"I want our children in America to know the limits of your achievements is the reach of your dreams and your willingness to work for them."*

This reflection joins hope to discipline. It affirms aspiration, but insists that effort and responsibility—not entitlement—are the means by which dreams are fulfilled.

> *"I have always admired quiet yet unwavering devotion to children — especially foster youth who are so often overlooked."*

This sentence captures the spirit of her service. It reveals a preference for constancy over recognition and for caring for those least likely to be seen.

◆ On Unity and Diversity

> *"Our strength, as a nation, comes from our diversity and we should celebrate our differences to make us stronger and kinder."*

Spoken without rancor, this remark frames unity not as uniformity, but as mutual respect. It reflects an understanding that cohesion grows when differences are acknowledged without hostility.

> **"As citizens of this great nation, it is kindness, love, and compassion for each other that will bring us together — and keep us together."**

This statement echoes a moral rather than political vision of unity. It places endurance not in ideology, but in character exercised toward one another.

◆ On Character and Promise

> **"Your word is your bond, and you do what you say and keep your promise."**

This principle reflects a traditional ethic of honor. In an era of shifting narratives, she affirmed that integrity begins with fidelity to one's word.

> **"Work hard for what you want in life."**

Simple and unembellished, this sentence reinforces a belief that effort precedes reward. It aligns with her own journey—marked by discipline, perseverance, and self-command.

> **"I prefer to show my values through my work."**

This statement stands as the quiet thesis of her public life. It explains her restraint, her avoidance of theatrics, and her enduring focus on action over rhetoric.

◆ Closing Reflection

Taken together, these words form a portrait of consistency. They reveal a woman who understood that leadership need not be loud to be effective, and that compassion, when practiced steadily, becomes a form of strength.

Melania Trump's voice—measured, restrained, and purposeful—does not seek to persuade through force. It endures through example.

> *"I prefer to show my values through my work."*

This statement captures the governing principle of her public life. In an age accustomed to declaration and display, she chose action. Her legacy rests not on rhetoric, but on sustained effort carried out without spectacle.

> **"My first priority is being a mother."**

Spoken without apology, this affirmation reflects a moral hierarchy often dismissed but rarely disproven. For Melania

Trump, motherhood was not in competition with public responsibility; it was its foundation. From this priority flowed her discipline, restraint, and focus on children as a sacred trust.

"I stay true to myself and my values."

This remark reveals the interior strength that sustained her under prolonged scrutiny. Rather than reshaping herself to satisfy shifting expectations, she remained anchored in conscience. Authenticity, for her, was not expressive—it was steadfast.

"You cannot walk away from your values."

This conviction explains her consistency. Values were not accessories to be adjusted under pressure, but commitments to be honored regardless of circumstance. Her life demonstrates that restraint and fidelity often speak more clearly than reaction.

"Be best."

Simple in language, demanding in practice. This phrase was never meant as branding, but as guidance—calling children, families, and society toward responsibility, dignity, and moral formation. Its strength lay in its simplicity, and its endurance in its intention.

These words, taken together, form a portrait of leadership grounded not in volume, but in virtue. They do not seek to persuade through force; they endure through example.

Scriptural Appendix

Throughout this book, Scripture has been used not to speculate, but to illuminate—offering parallels that help interpret a life marked by restraint, service, and quiet strength. The following passages align naturally with the themes present in Melania Trump's journey.

◆ **John 14:12**

> *"Whoever believes in me will do the works that I do, and will do greater ones than these..."*

This passage reflects the dignity of work done in faith, even when unnoticed. It affirms that lasting impact is not measured by visibility, but by fidelity to purpose—an echo of Melania Trump's preference for action over acclaim.

◆ **Matthew 25:40**

> *"Whatever you did for one of the least of these brothers and sisters of mine, you did for me."*

This verse resonates with her focus on children, the vulnerable, and those who serve quietly. It frames compassion not as sentiment, but as moral responsibility—offered without expectation of return.

◆ **Luke 2:51**

> *"And his mother treasured all these things in her heart."*

Mary's silent guardianship provides a fitting parallel to Melania Trump's discipline of privacy and protection. This verse honors the strength found in watchfulness, restraint, and faithful presence.

◆ Proverbs 31 (Selected Verses)

Selected verses from Proverbs 31 speak to dignity without display, strength tempered by wisdom, and honor earned over time:

> *"Strength and dignity are her clothing, and she laughs at the time to come."*

> *"She opens her mouth with wisdom, and the teaching of kindness is on her tongue."*
> *"Her children rise up and call her blessed."*

These passages do not describe ambition, but character—virtue exercised daily, often unseen. They offer a timeless framework through which to understand a legacy shaped by order, discipline, and enduring grace.

◆ Closing Note

This back matter does not seek to conclude the story, but to steady it. Quotes and Scripture serve here as witnesses—not to spectacle, but to substance. They remind the reader that a life lived with restraint often leaves the deepest imprint.

In Melania Trump's example, words were few, actions deliberate, and values constant. That harmony, once achieved, requires no further defense.

I want our children
in America to know
the limits of your
achievements is the
reach of your dreams
and your willingness
to work for them.

– First Lady
  Melania Trump

Colophon

This book was written and prepared with care, restraint, and intention.

The text was composed by **Joe Hung Nguyen**, drawing upon historical record, reflection, Scripture, and poetic meditation. The manuscript was formatted in a classic serif typeface to ensure clarity, longevity, and readability across print editions.

Design choices favored simplicity and white space, allowing words to carry meaning without distraction. Quotation watermarks and section dividers were selected to reinforce theme rather than ornament, and all visual elements were chosen to serve the text quietly.

This volume was created to endure—not to persuade, but to bear witness to character, dignity, and a life shaped by disciplined action.

Author's Closing Letter to the Reader

To every reader who has taken the time to open this book, I offer my sincere gratitude.

This work was created not to persuade, but to preserve. It is intended as a reference—a steady record for libraries, shelves, and future generations who may wish to understand a First Lady whose public presence was often quiet, yet consistently purposeful.

Throughout her years in the White House, Melania Trump carried out her role with restraint, composure, and intention. She chose her words carefully. She expressed herself more through action than through speech. Her initiatives for children, including *Be Best* and other compassionate efforts, reflected a commitment to well-being that extended beyond borders and beyond attention.

Her public life unfolded during a period marked by intense scrutiny and uncommon challenge. As a wife, a mother, and a First Lady, she navigated circumstances that tested privacy, resolve, and family life. Through these moments, she remained steady—a quality that has become central to her legacy.

This book draws upon historical record, reflection, Scripture, and poetic meditation. Its purpose is simple: to bear witness to character, dignity, and a life shaped by disciplined action.

If these pages help readers see her more clearly—not through the lens of praise or criticism, but through the lens of truth, context, and quiet strength—then this work has fulfilled its intention.

Thank you for reading.
Thank you for reflecting.

And thank you for allowing this book to become part of your understanding of a First Lady whose legacy continues to unfold.

With respect,

Joe Hung Nguyen
Deacon, a refugee from Vietnam

www.ingramcontent.com/pod-product-compliance
Lightning Source LLC
Chambersburg PA
CBHW020759130626
46554CB00006B/2264